THE SAAS SALES METHOD

FOR SALES DEVELOPMENT REPRESENTATIVES:

How to Prospect for Customers

BY JACCO VAN DER KOOIJ
AND DAN SMITH

Edited by Fernando Pizarro and Dan Smith

Revision 5.0

ISBN-13: 978-1986270656

ISBN-10: 1986270653

Winning by Design LLC
San Francisco, California
United States of America
For more information, visit www.winningbydesign.com

More from Winning by Design

The SaaS Sales Method for Sales Development Representatives: How to Prospect for Customers is part of Winning by Design's Sales Blueprints series. Other books in the series include:

The SaaS Sales Method: The Science and Process of Sales

Blueprints for a SaaS Sales Organization: How to Design, Build and Scale a Customer-Centric Sales Organization

The SaaS Sales Method Fundamentals: How to Have Customer Conversations

The SaaS Sales Method for Account Executives: How to Win Customers

The SaaS Sales Method for Customer Success & Account Managers: How to Grow Customers

Contents

Introduction

In modern sales organizations, prospecting requires the sales professional to provide value from the first interaction. Most companies generally break this team into a separate function or job title. Whether the role is called a Sales Development Rep (SDR), an Inside Sales Rep (ISR), Business Development Rep (BDR) or Account Development Rep (ADR) the function is similar and includes all the activities required to find and qualify prospects and prepare them for the selling process (which we cover in a subsequent book). This book is designed to outline those activities and provide you with best practices, and we will primarily use SDR to represent the person primarily implementing these activities.

NOTE: This book is meant to get dirty! We encourage you to write in it, do the exercises, dog-ear the pages, and do anything else that will help you interact with the content.

A brief review of customer engagement

In *The SaaS Sales Method Fundamentals: How to Have Customer Conversations*, we discuss how to have conversations in a variety of interactions. Now we are going to turn a variety of interactions in a series of sequences. Predefined sequences we can repeat are called **Plays**.

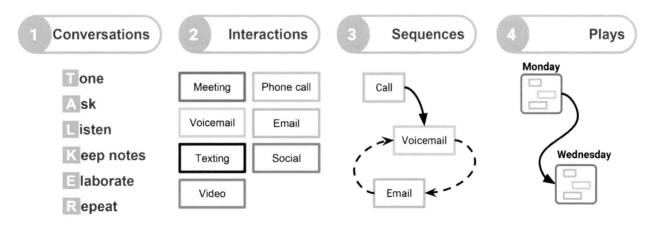

Figure 1: Initiating conversations through interactions, sequences and plays

Four different ways of prospecting

Prospecting can take many different forms, but generally falls into four categories we have placed on the customer journey below.

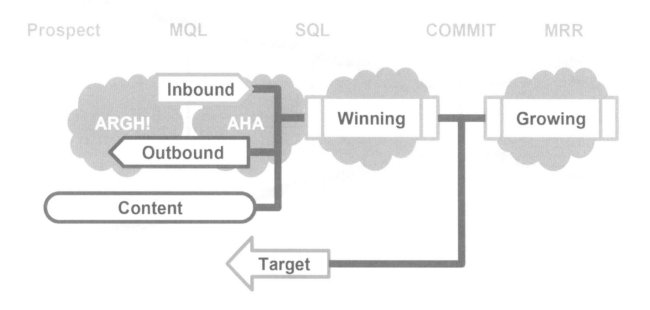

Figure 2: Overview of the prospecting processes along the customer journey

INBOUND	Customers educate themselves and seek assistance in the selection process.
OUTBOUND	Volume-based outbound through a cadence of personalized touches.
TARGETED	Targeting a number of people in a specific account, also known as Account-based Marketing (ABM) and Account-based Prospecting (ABP).
CONTENT	Educate customers through content on both the problem as well as the solution.

Customer-centric qualification

In Figure 2, you will notice there are several measurement points along the journey. These measurement points can be used as criteria to determine whether a lead is qualified. We have listed some common qualification criteria in Table 1.

Traditional qualification used BANT™, CHAMP™, or MEDDIC™, all processes in which customers are asked if they have Budget, are the Decision Maker, have a Need, are working to a Timeline, and so on. These qualification methods do not apply in a customer-centric approach because the customer gains no value during the qualification process, often leading to the customer being standoffish.

Table 1 Progressions of leads as they develop

Criteria	Prospect	MQL	SQL	SAL
Lead profile is a fit (Problem matches solution)	YES	YES	YES	YES
Lead expresses interest in learning more (Educate)		YES	YES	YES
Lead is interested in talking to an expert			YES	YES
Lead has a critical event/defined impact				YES

- **Prospect:** A person who expresses interest online.
- **MQL:** Marketing Qualified Lead, a person who expresses interest and fits the profile.
- **SQL:** Sales Qualified Lead, a person who expresses interest during the sales process.
- **SAL:** Sales Accepted Lead, is a Marketing Qualified Lead (MQL) that has been reviewed and passed to the sales team for approval.

EXERCISE: **Identify the criteria that might make a lead fit to be a PROSPECT**

Criteria can be static, such as company size. They can be time-driven, such as an event experienced. Or they can be based on the prospect's current situation, such as infrastructure they have in place. There are many other potential criteria! Try out your own below.

CRITERIA 1: .... CRITERIA 4: ....

CRITERIA 2: .... CRITERIA 5: ....

CRITERIA 3: .... CRITERIA 6: ....

 **PRO TIP** Don't qualify your customer, but see if they are a good fit. Looking for fit is like asking if they have the right profile for you to impact (improve) their business. If you can have a big impact, priority and budget will follow. But your solution is not for everyone.

- DOMINIQUE LEVIN

1   Inbound

During inbound lead development, you need to take the right action based on the quality of the lead, since quality can vary a lot.

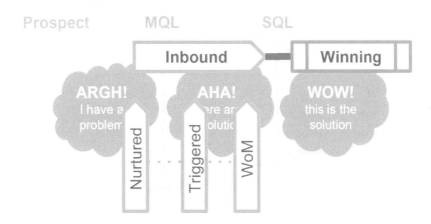

Figure 3: Overview of the Inbound prospecting processes along the customer journey

The three most common prospecting processes are:

1. **Nurtured:** Prospects from the contact database have been "cookied." When they visit your website and download content, they gain "points." Once they achieve a certain "nurture value" or "lead score" based on those points, your sales platform generates an inbound lead. This process is heavily skewed to whether the lead downloads a white paper or signs up to a webinar. We recommend that a nurtured lead should also be fed into the outbound process.

2. **Alerted:** An alert on the website (most commonly: contact sales, request demo) generates an inbound lead. **The development rep** needs to follow up promptly and schedule a discovery call. With this type of lead, all the development rep has to say is "How may I help you?"

3. **Word of Mouth (WoM):** A new customer hears about you via word-of-mouth. These are the hottest leads! And they need to be properly managed, which means sometimes they should go straight to the Account Executive (AE) for selling (see *The SaaS Sales Method: The Science and Process of Sales*

4.).

1.1 Alerted

An alerted inbound lead is also referred to as an MQL where the SDR will interact with the prospect to try and book a meeting. MQLs can come from a variety of sources including website, events, social media etc. Sometimes a single action is not enough to turn a suspect into a prospect. For example, if a customer visits your pricing page once. But if you noticed they went to your pricing page, downloaded a white paper and visited your website 3 times in a one week, they may be qualified to have a conversation. For your business, identify some of these actions in the exercise below.

EXERCISE: **Identify the alerting actions that made a lead into a Marketing Qualified Lead (MQL)**

For example, an action can be the download of a white paper or repeated visits to the pricing page.

ACTION 1: .... ACTION 4: ....

ACTION 2: .... ACTION 5: ....

ACTION 3: .... ACTION 6: Exceeded Nurture Value

Reach out to the customer with either a SingleTap or DoubleTap Play.

Winning By Design SingleTap™ Inbound Engagement Play

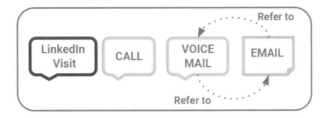

Winning By Design DoubleTap™ Inbound Engagement Play

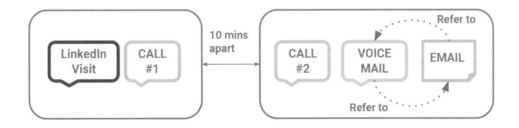

STEP 1 LINKEDIN VISIT

- Visit the person's LinkedIn profile (we could can say more here, but that's pretty much it).

STEP 2 CALL THEM

- Place call #1 at 10-15 minutes before the top of the hour (most people have meetings that start at the top of the hour).

- Place call #2 a few minutes after call #1; this indicates that you are trying to get hold of them. Make the calls at least 4-5 minutes apart (1-2 minutes apart often indicates an emergency from a partner, family member, etc.).

Good morning {{first name}}, how are you doing? This is ____ from ___. We received your inquiry for ____ on _____ and I am reaching out to learn how I can help.

STEP 3 **LEAVE A VOICEMAIL – If not answered, leave a voicemail (and refer to the email)**

Hello Mary,

This is Mike from XYZ.

I am responding to your inquiry for more information.

Mary, I will send you an email, but in case you prefer to reach out via phone my number is 123-456-7890.

Again, this is Mike from XYZ, and my phone number is 123-456-7890.

Looking forward to hearing from you Mary!

STEP 4 **EMAIL THEM – Follow the voicemail instantly with an email (which refers to the voicemail)**

Hello Mary

Just left you a voicemail in response to your request. Let me know how I can help. You can hit reply or call me back at 123-456-7890.

Looking forward to hearing from you Mary.

John

PS: Here is a <great article> you may like based on what I read about you on LinkedIn

{{Email signature with company name, links to blog posts, phone number, etc.}}

Key Takeaways:

- Open immediately by addressing "Why are you calling/emailing me?"

- Let them know you sent a voicemail, signalling that you are persistent.

- Call-to-action in the close – "Looking forward" – tells Mary she needs to take action.

- The PS: This is used to communicate an article which allows John to have an opening chat about it in their call later on.

- Email signature tells "who is calling."

INBOUND EXERCISE: **Create a SingleTap Sequence**

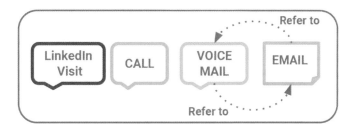

STEP 1 **Pick a person and VISIT their LinkedIn Profile**

STEP 2 **Write out the opening CALL (Use opening from** *The SaaS Sales Method Fundamentals: How to Have Customer Conversations***)**

STEP 3 **Write out the VOICEMAIL (Use WWW from** *The SaaS Sales Method Fundamentals: How to Have Customer Conversations***)**

STEP 4 **Draft the EMAIL (Use RRR format from** *The SaaS Sales Method Fundamentals: How to Have Customer Conversations*)

1.2 Nurtured

A nurtured inbound is in many cases referred to as a Marketing Qualified Lead. Nurtured inbound can be anywhere from "Just learned about this for the first time" to "I may need help right now!"

When nurturing a customer, make sure your communication always provides something of value. Don't "Check in" or "bubble up my last message" – if you're only asking for a meeting, you are not giving them anything in exchange.

1.2 EXERCISE: **Come up with a list of actions that customers can take on your website:**

Action can be request a demo, contact sales etc.

ACTION 1: Contact Sales / Request Demo   ACTION 4: ....

ACTION 2: ....   ACTION 5: ....

ACTION 3: ....   ACTION 6: ....

In response to a nurtured inbound, we recommend a hyper-relevant message as described in *The SaaS Sales Method Fundamentals: How to Have Customer Conversations.*

1.3 Inbound from Word of Mouth

Word of Mouth is the most powerful form of inbound and requires your utmost attention to address the needs of not just the customer, but also the referrer.

EXAMPLE: **The inbound**

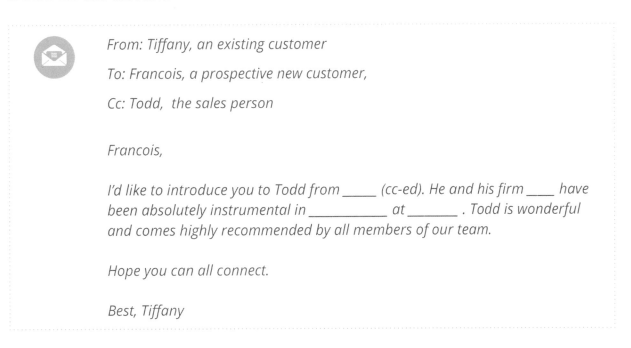

From: Tiffany, an existing customer

To: Francois, a prospective new customer,

Cc: Todd, the sales person

Francois,

I'd like to introduce you to Todd from _____ (cc-ed). He and his firm ____ have been absolutely instrumental in _____ at _____ . Todd is wonderful and comes highly recommended by all members of our team.

Hope you can all connect.

Best, Tiffany

STEP 1 **Reach out to your WoM source to express appreciation and ask any specifics (be quick)**

STEP 2 **Research your prospective customer! (5-10 minutes)**

STEP 3 Reach out to customer via email and offer a call

From: Todd, the sales person

To: Francois, a prospective new customer,

Bcc: Tiffany, an existing customer

Thank you Tiffany, I will move you to bcc to preserve your inbox.

Francois,

Nice to meet you. I've done some research and notice ___ and ___. Would love to learn more. When is a good time to talk for you?

With kind regards,

Todd

PS: Here is some valuable insight based on my research: ___

IMPORTANT: A Word of Mouth reference requires you to double up on all your effort, e.g.; a quicker response, more research, better use of words, more relevant use-cases etc. Do not forget to thank the "giver." You may even reward with a Starbucks gift card.

1.4 Social Inbound Play

SOCIAL INBOUND PLAY In a social selling inbound play, your customer is visiting your profile, often in response to your blogging, sharing or simply because you reached out to them. They are checking out your chops.

Reaching out to a customer in follow-up to a social activity

STEP 1 Prepare

Make sure your LinkedIn Profile offers value, looks professional, shows you to be authentic, and reflects that you are an expert.

STEP 2 Research to identify something relevant!

Visit their LinkedIn profile and identify what is relevant to them, then find some insights for them.

STEP 3 Reach out with gratitude

Ashley – Thanks for stopping by. Love your LI profile! Let me know if you found any of the information valuable.

Based on your background, I thought you'd appreciate this article <LINK>.

Considering your work, I think you will like the 2nd paragraph outlining how events are the cornerstone of Marketing these days. Aimee

STEP 4 **Sent out LinkedIn Connect Request**

Ashley – In follow-up to our conversation on _____. Would love to connect and share insights as they become available. Aimee

BEST PRACTICES

- DO thank them for stopping by!

- **DO NOT** sell or ask for a meeting. Period.

- DO offer valuable insight – it does not have to come from you or your company!

- DO keep it very short – you are texting!

- **DO NOT** lead with "social" relevance such as Alma Mater – you haven't earned that yet!

2   Outbound

Outbound prospecting can take place across all three customer experiences.

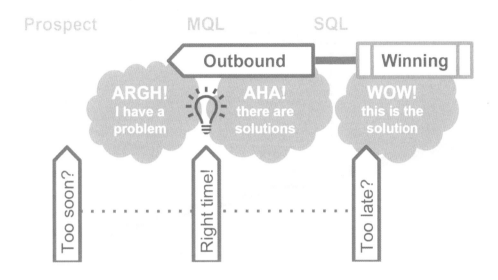

Figure 4: Depiction of where Outbound prospecting happens along the customer journey

Figure 4 shows that the most effective time for outbound marketing occurs between what we term the "ARGH" and "AHA" stages.

ARGH: Customers in the "Argh! I have a problem" stage means they have a problem you could potentially solve. Sometimes customers are not even aware they have this problem. Finding customers who are a fit to have you help them solve the problem, and if they can benefit from the impact your solution provides should be a priority for them.

- PRO: Customers are very open-minded.

- CON: It can take a long time to educate. They don't understand it yet.

- **WHEN:** If you are selling to top-tier enterprise accounts and expect about 10-20 high-value deals per year, perform a provocative outbound sales process. This is the most complex type of outbound to do effectively.

AHA: Customers who already have experienced the problem, but did not know a solution existed, or maybe have heard about some solutions but were unable to spend time on it yet.

- **PRO:** Customers are still a bit open-minded; they understand some of the impact.

- **CON:** You are unaware if they need 2 more weeks or months of education (Critical Event).

- **WHEN:** In case you need to win dozens of deals a month (SMB/Mid Market).

WOW: Customers who are price shopping for vendors and are comparing offerings, sometimes even feature-by-feature.

- **PRO:** Customers are ready to move forward quickly.

- **CON:** Customers are looking for the best price/performance solution.

- **WHEN:** If you need to win hundreds of deals a month (often low acv, VSB).

We recognize four different kind of outbound techniques:

- **HYPER-RELEVANT:** Address one specific person you hand-picked.

- **GROUP-RELEVANT:** Address a group of people who all experience the same "challenge."

- **EVENT-BASED:** Invite a person/group of people to an educational event.

- **CONTENT-BASED:** Share insights with a person/group of people over time.

There are three dimensions in outbound prospecting:

- **Ideal Customer Profile (ICP):** Different person, different value prop.

- **Day/Time Window:** Response rates can vary significantly based on the day and the time.

- **Contents:** Subject line, opening, and structure of the email will impact response to an email.

1-Dimensional: Taps	2-Dimensional: Days	3-Dimensional: People
X	$X * Y$	$X * Y * Z$
Number of Taps (x)	Number of Taps (X) across Days (Y)	Number of Taps (X) across Days (Y)
		Addressing different ICPs (Z) in a single account
Example:	*Example: (7x21)*	*Example: (7x35x3)*
A single RRR email or a SingleTap	7 touches across 21 days	7 touches across 35 days addressing 3 roles.
Common Use-case:	**Common Use-case:**	**Common Use-case:**
Inbound	Outbound 1: Few	Account-Based Marketing
Outbound 1-1	Event	

2.1 One-to-One Outbound Prospecting (1:1)

You can deliver a hyper-relevant outbound message with a SingleTap. We do NOT recommend a DoubleTap, as the customer has not expressed a sense of urgency.

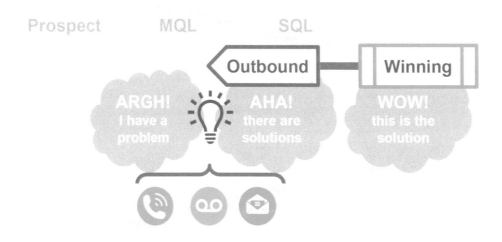

Figure 5: Depiction of hyper-relevant Outbound message

To be hyper-relevant you have to be:

- WHEN **At the right** time – e.g. person was just hired as the new VP in charge, and sits right at the AHA moment.

- WHAT **On the right** topic – e.g. "we noticed you were hiring 10 new QA Engineers."

- WHERE **In the right** context – e.g. "have you considered outsourcing QA to increase speed?"

EXAMPLE: Hyper-relevant RRR message

Subject: Congrats / Insights for VP CSM / Here to help

Hi Jennifer,

Congratulations on the new role as VP of Customer Success last week. We would like to welcome you with the attached ebook on the most common challenges a VP of CSM experiences.

Jennifer, you may in particular enjoy page 2 where John Doe, with whom you are connected, talks about the three challenges he ran into.

Let me know if you like me to keep you apprised on the latest in CSM?

Best - Nashimi

PRO TIP The difference between an email that gets opened and SPAM is the effort you put into creating relevance and providing thoughtful insights.

-- DAN SMITH

I. To be hyper-relevant you must understand different impact propositions

The impact your solution creates differs for each hierarchical layer in a target company. You need to understand the different impact propositions as they relate to your service.

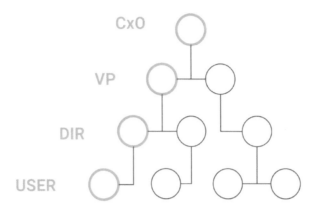

Figure 6: Persona title totem pole

EXERCISE: What is the value your product/service provides per persona

ICP/Role	Persona-Based Impact Proposition	Where They Get Their Info
	Fill in:	*Fill in (LI, Quora, Medium, Twitter, FB):*
(e.g. CEO)		
	Fill in:	*Fill in (Tradeshows, peers, webinars):*
(e.g. VP)		
	Fill in:	*Fill in (Tradeshows, peers, webinars):*

STEP 1 **What are the sample titles of your target audience?**

(e.g., Chief Customer Officer, Creative Talent Manager, Inside Sales Manager, etc.)

.... [Title]

.... [Title]

.... [Title]

.... [Title]

.... [Title]

STEP 2 **Develop an understanding of the person**

Create a description of the persona by researching their LinkedIn profile in detail:

- Who are they (hobbies, personality, family status, etc.).

- What content do they like (video, white paper, books, etc.).

- Where do they get their information (LinkedIn, Quora, newsletters, LinkedIn groups, Twitter, etc.).

Example	Visit LinkedIn Profile
Jody J @ ACME	Name:
• VP Marketing	• ....
• Female mid 40s	• ....
• On LinkedIn and Twitter	• ....
• Loves video content and infographics	• ....
• Tweets about 4-5/week	• ....
• Part of LinkedIn group x, y and z	• ....
• Video on YouTube: xxxxx	• ....
• Blog posts on topics: yyyyyy	• ....

STEP 3 Obtain contact information

Obtaining contact data is not as hard as it seems. Google Chrome extensions like Email Hunter (https://emailhunter.co/) provide you with a customer's email address by checking the database of email syntaxes. Also check www.mailtester.com to double-check or find others.

Research your ICP

If you know more about the customer, the impact and consequences of the imminent decision – and you have the right solution – you will win! This power is earned by thorough online research, which signals to your customer that you care about them.

II. Four plays to engage with an ideal customer

As you approach an account, you need a blueprint – a plan that outlines what to do. In this section, we outline a variety of plays to use for engaging with an account.

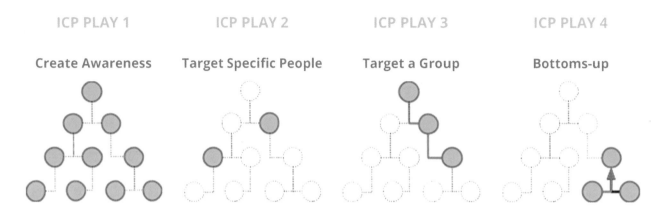

ICP PLAY 1 Awareness - Visit all relevant LinkedIn profiles

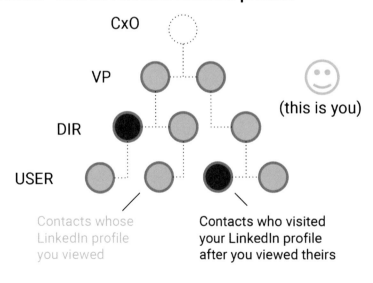

Figure 7: Summary of ICP Plays

Great for these situations:

- First touch

- Right before a call

- Establishing awareness in a key account

Pros:

- Easy to do

- Automate using tools

- Non-intrusive

Cons: Need a level of insight/intelligence

Visit the LinkedIn profiles of each target person at the account. By visiting these profiles, you are establishing brand awareness as they visit their "Who viewed me" page (but before you do this, make sure you have set up your LinkedIn profile to be customer-centric!). In the figure above, you see that you visited all profiles and that four people visited you back. Those people can be addressed with an outbound email: In this case, you can send a message to the VP.

"Dear ____, Thank you for visiting my profile, hope the insights were of use..." (see social inbound play in paragraph 1.4)

ICP PLAY 2-1 **Go Direct – reach out directly – Use RRR**

Great for these situations:

- When you found the right person

- Right before a call/email

- Right after a call/email

- After play 1

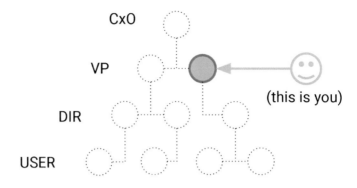

Pros:

- Effective when done right

Figure 8: Go Direct Play with email

Cons:

- Requires research

- Can be intrusive when not done right

In this approach, you target a senior executive directly following extensive research.

EXAMPLE: Quick direct message to a senior person

Subject: Per your CEO

Andy – Your CEO {{full name}} stated that he has quadrupled your goal for next year. Your peer {{full name}} at {{company name}} had the exact same challenge. Let me know if I can send you his insights on how he did it!

Best,
Cam

EXAMPLE: Using a list of "Top 40 under 40" that is awarded annually in many major cities (Using RRR)

Subject: Congrats! / Your Growth Initiative / Meet next week

{{Opening}},

Congratulations! on being named to the Top 40 under 40; it looks like you are knocking it out of the park.

Your sales director, {{person x}}, and {{person y}} on your team, are evaluating our solution for your marketing initiative this quarter.

Since this is a new initiative for {{company name}}, my team encouraged me to share some of the best practices {{link to article}}. Specifically the 4th paragraph which discusses {{relevant value prop}}.

{{First name}}, assuming you are tied up with quarter-end this week, how does your schedule look for early next week to have a call about the progress so far?

Best,
Jackie

ICP PLAY 2-2 **Go Direct – reach out based on a social activity**

In a social selling outreach, you are using an activity on social media to start a conversation. The key here is that your aim is to start a conversation by providing them more insights! NOT to set up a meeting.

EXAMPLE: **A prospective customer recently blogged about the lack of engagement at a trade show**

STEP 1 **Prepare**

 Make sure your LinkedIn Profile offers value, looks professional, shows you to be authentic, and reflects that you are an expert.

STEP 2 **Research to identify something relevant!**

 Visit their LinkedIn profile (again). This time look close, qualify if this is a fit, and identify what is relevant to them. Then find a relevant insight that helps them.

STEP 3 **Place a call (remember they're thinking "Who are you, why are you calling, what's in it for me?")**

Hello John – this is Aimee how are you?

Doing alright Aimee ...what is this about?

*Well John, I just **read** your blog post on LinkedIn. I loved it.*

Thank you Aimee.

What stood out was how you shared the importance of engagement.

May I ask what inspired you to write that?

Ohh it is something I am passionate about.

Same here! I love to share this article with you that

provides more insights into ... can I send this to you?

***Yes** why not...*

- DO address: Who you are, Why are you calling, and What's in it for them.

- DO use different forms of reaching out, such as call, voicemail, email.

- DO compliment / applaud their work.

- **DO NOT** refer to you "seeing," "noticing," or "hearing about."

- DO mention you READ the article.

- DO call out a specific section that stood out.

- **DO NOT** sell or ask for a meeting. Period.

- DO offer insights, and/or access to an expert on the topic in question.

ICP PLAY 2-3 **Vertical Approach – Group target, using CEO statement to light a fire**

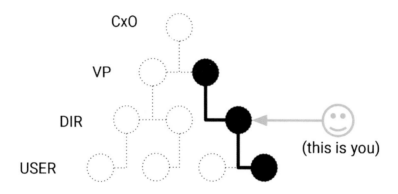

Figure 9: Vertical approach aligning through executive priorities

Great for these situations:

- Individuals are not responding to you.

- Unclear to you who is doing what.

- Event invites.

- After play 1 and play 2.

Pros:

- Effective when done right.
- Get a quick response.

Cons:

- Can be very intrusive when not done right.
- Difficult to automate.

EXAMPLE: **Email to multiple people (Using RRR)**

When you address multiple people, you cc: the most senior person. What will happen is that the person responsible will respond to you.

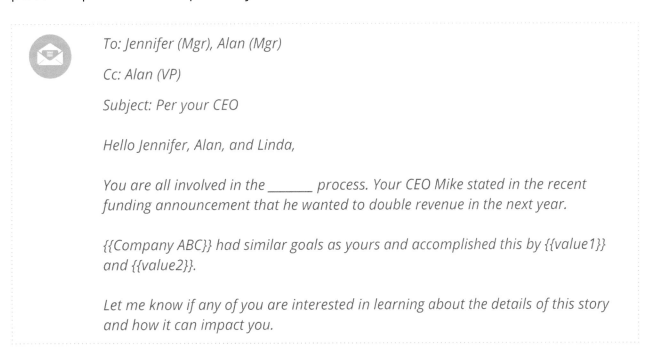

To: Jennifer (Mgr), Alan (Mgr)

Cc: Alan (VP)

Subject: Per your CEO

Hello Jennifer, Alan, and Linda,

You are all involved in the _____ process. Your CEO Mike stated in the recent funding announcement that he wanted to double revenue in the next year.

{{Company ABC}} had similar goals as yours and accomplished this by {{value1}} and {{value2}}.

Let me know if any of you are interested in learning about the details of this story and how it can impact you.

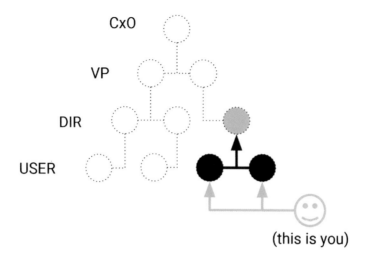

Figure 10: Bottoms-up approach

Great for these situations:

- When you offer a user-driven service (such as a Chrome extension) and want to gain a foothold.

Pros:

- Fault tolerant: e.g. you have lots of users to practice on.

Cons:

- Takes a long time to get to a decision maker.

In this approach, you target the actual users of your target company's product. You can target them directly (via the RRR method) or indirectly:

- Comment on a blog post/tweet, like, share etc.

- Publish your own blog post, then share it with them (can ask a mutual connection to forward).

III. Multithreading: Creating a broader platform once you have the meeting

Within larger accounts, often multiple people are responsible for the same area. This allows you to create a broader platform inside an account that goes beyond just one person, one group, or one division. You can do this by contacting those from other groups and involving them in the meeting.

STEP 1 **Secure the meeting**

STEP 2 **Invite others to the meeting**

Five ways to invite others to the meeting:

1. Ask your sponsor: *"Danny, who else can benefit from attending the meeting on Friday?"*

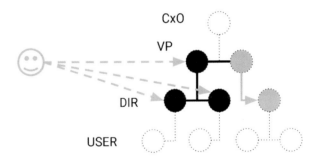

Figure 11: Multi-thread communications

2. Mention others you think can benefit: *"I think Mary and John could benefit from this meeting. Danny, do you think you can invite them?"*

3. Just straight up invite Mary and John: *"Mary/John – We are meeting next week with Danny at department Y. I thought you could benefit from this meeting. Would you like to attend?"*

4. Share with Danny what others have done: *"Danny, other companies I've worked with have found that inviting others in these kind of roles benefited greatly. I notice that Mary and John are in these positions. Do you think you can invite them?"*

5. Call John and Mary by phone and invite them personally – have a conversation! (BE CAREFUL)

STEP 3 **Send out the invitations**

If your meeting does not result in a deal, you at least have created alternative paths. We recommend that, when you invite other departments, you mention who you are working with, so they can contact them.

PRO TIP: Over the years, we have heard far too often that people restrict themselves from expanding their footprint without guidance from their champion, because once in the past, it backfired. However, it is rare that it backfires. Reach out – there's very little risk, and you won't know until you try!

– JACCO VAN DER KOOIJ

2.2 Group-Based Outbound

Creating hyper-relevant messages for a single person is time consuming and not efficient. You simply do not have enough time to create these. This means you have to create them in volume by addressing a topic that is relevant to them.

1. Instead of hyper-relevant emails sent to a single person, you send it to a group acting as a cohort.

2. The cadence contains those in the cohort with a series of emails/calls/touches.

3. You are developing conversations with several people in the cohort.

4. We secure online meetings with qualified prospects (who behave as cohorts).

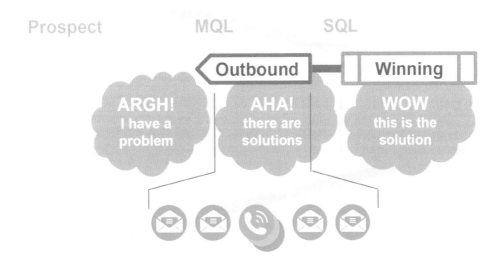

Figure 12: Overview of the Outbound prospecting processes along the customer journey

There are several key principles in group outbound prospecting.

You must be relevant to the group (The What)

You can get even better results when you plan per "vertical" – also known as "sprints." In each sprint, we focus on just one vertical market, allowing us to optimize on the use-case knowledge, as well as get educated on the particulars of that vertical market (specific competitors, partners, etc.). When sending out emails to more than one person at a time, it is important to make sure the group is not too big – 10-25 people is ideal. Rarely should sales people send out batch emails to 100+ people at a time – leave this to your marketing team.

Table 2 Group outbound prospecting

Tap	(E) or (R)	Insight provided
Email 1	Emotional	Provide a vision-based video that points out a better tomorrow.
Email 2	Emotional	A link to a "scientist on a white board" explaining things.
SingleTap	Emotional/ Rational	Invite to webinar with a third-party expert.
Email 4	Rational	Provide an analyst report.
Email 5	Rational	Invite to meet with expert to see in action.

EXAMPLE: A group of 10 VPs of Sales at cyber-security companies that have between 200-500 employees. Recently, new legislation came out that they need to know about. You are able to send them a similar email because you know the message is likely to resonate.

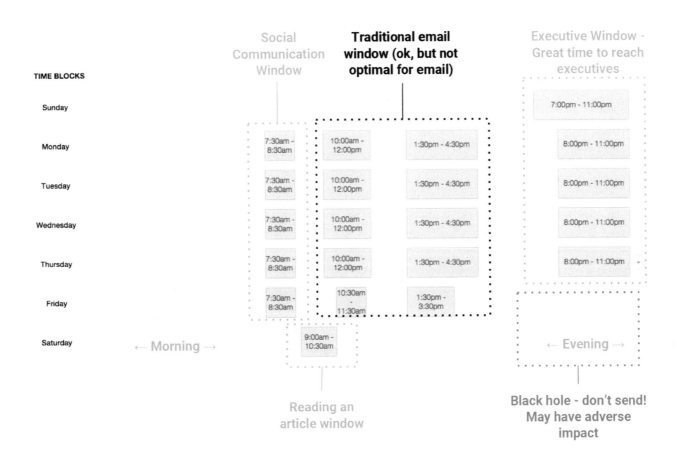

Figure 13: Optimal time windows for communication

Across different channels (The Where)

Email is not your only channel. There are many alternative channels to consider.

Channel	Soft touch	Soft touch	Hard touch
Twitter	Follow, Like, Retweet	Mention	Direct Message
LinkedIn	Follow, Like, Share	Comment, Mention	Connect
Facebook	Like, Share	Comment	Befriend
Instagram	Love, Follow	Comment	Refer in other medium
Quora	Upvote, Follow	Comment	Refer in article

You need to learn how your personas across the organization discover content. Why? Because you want to reach people with information in ways that they like to consume it. If that's how they like to absorb information, then the chances are greater that they will engage. Similarly, the value prop differs for each hierarchical layer in a target company. You need to understand the different value props as they relate to your service.

Group	Group Value Proposition	Where They Get Their Info
Role	*Fill in:*	
	....	....
	....	....
Vertical	*Fill in:*	
	....	....
	....	....
Account	*Fill in:*	
	....	....
	....	....
Problem	*Fill in:*	
	....	....
	....	....

1-to-Few Plays

The key to great cadence structure that results in Sales Qualified Leads (SQLs) is knowing your audience and how they expect to interact with you. Whether or not your prospect ends up buying from you, you can earn their respect and trust by providing value. Here's proven sequencing that drives meetings, but it is always evolving. Try one of these, and then test a new flow to see if it works better for your ICPs.

1 to FEW PLAY 1 **7x15 Educate Play**

Who: This is optimized for: Identified group of prospects that have a similar problem.

What: 7 touches over 14 days across different days. Email heavy, with an easy phone call where you give (not take) an invite to a webinar.

When: Used often.

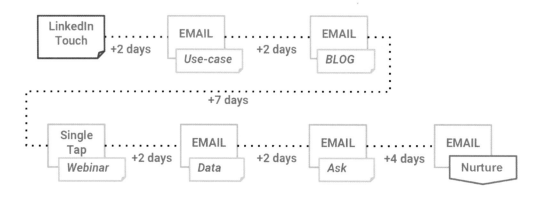

Figure 14: Educate Play

Breakdown:

Week 1

- **Monday**: Prepare the group you will address; this includes a LinkedIn soft touch.

- **Tuesday**: Introduction email – RRR with use-case.

- **Thursday**: Add value email – provide reference to a blog post.

Week 2

- **Monday**: Invite to a webinar.

- **Wednesday**: Connect on LinkedIn with a personalized note.

- **Friday**: Email with the ask – offer help of an expert.

Week 3

- **Monday**: Just busy or not interested followed by putting on a slow drip (once/month).

1-FEW PLAY 2 **8 x 24 FOMO Play**

Who: This is optimized to go cross-titles, but within the same vertical markets creating a fear of missing out by sharing lots of relatable customer success stories (e.g. within the vertical).

What: 7 emails, 3 calls, 3 voicemails, 1 LinkedIn visit.

When: This works really well with a vertical focus (or sprint) lead development program.

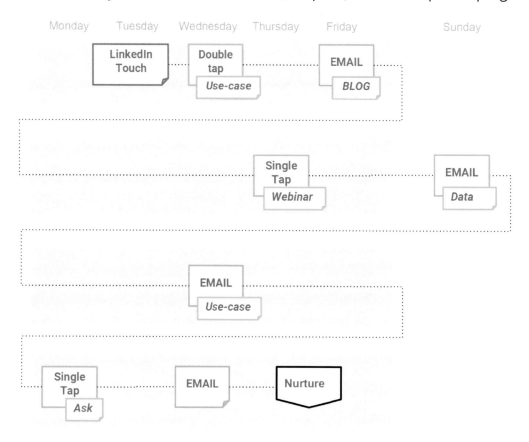

Figure 15: FOMO Play

Breakdown:

Week 1

- **Tuesday**: Research and visit LI profile.

- **Wednesday**: DoubleTap (Call//Call, Voicemail, Email #1) with relatable use-case.

- **Friday**: Send email sharing a blog post from a relatable customer.

Week 2

- **Thursday**: SingleTap with invite to webinar where a relatable customer speaks.

- **Sunday**: Email and share relatable customer use-case.

Week 3

- **Wednesday**: Email with a relatable customer use-case.

Week 4

- **Monday**: SingleTap with ask.

- **Wednesday**: Just busy or not interested followed by putting on a slow drip (once/month).

1-FEW PLAY 3 **7 x 35 Social Play**

Who: Optimized to go after the CxO who is active on social networks.

What: Several social touches spread over a longer period.

When: This works really well with an ABM program when you need to get to a specific person.

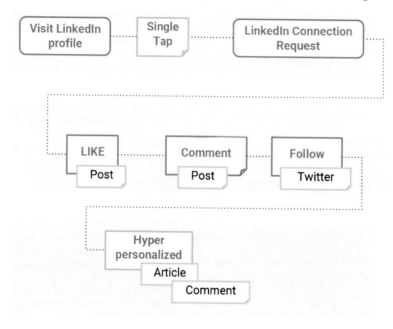

Figure 16: Social Play

Breakdown:

Week 1

- **Monday**: Visit LI profile.

- **Tuesday**: SingleTap.

- **Friday**: Social Touch.

Week 2/3/4

- Social Touch.

- Social Touch.

- Social Touch.

Week 5

- RRR Hyper-personalized email.

Code the plays:

EXAMPLE 1: **Dimensional 5 touch cadence – Double Tap Call (commonly used for inbound)**

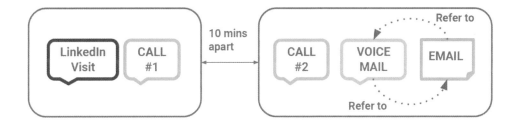

We can now code the plays:

VOICEMAIL: It's primary focus is to ask them to read your email

Hello Mary,

This is Mike from XYZ. I am trying to get hold of you to see if you are able to join the ABC event next week.

Mary, I've also sent you an email in case you prefer to communicate via email. Again this is Mike from XYZ, and my phone number is 123-456-7890; again, that's 123-456-7890. Bye.

EMAIL REFERRING TO THE VOICEMAIL: No longer a cold email

Hello Mary – I just left you a voicemail.

You recently asked us to keep you apprised. As it happens, we are organizing a get together of your peers this week to talk about XYZ. I am trying to get hold of you to see if you are able to join us.

Best,

John

EXAMPLE **16 x 21 Email/Call Cadence (commonly used for outbound)**

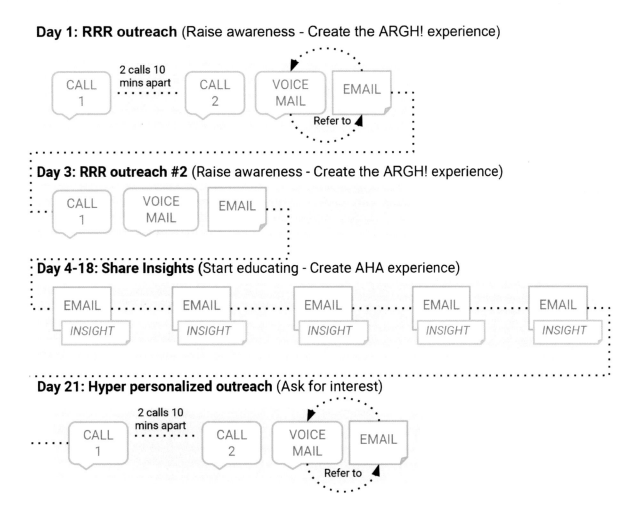

Figure 17: Example Play

Email Day One

Subject: Congrats/Scaling issues/Insights

Hi Jill,

Congrats on the recent round of Series C funding. I was prompted to reach out as I work with others like you, such as {{first name at company, and first name at company}} to help them scale their sales efforts.

HBR recently published an article on this topic (LINK), and I thought you would especially like this quote as it seems to relate: {{quote}}

Let me know if this is relevant and I will send you more insights on this topic!

Meghan

Email Day Three

Subject: In follow-up to my voicemail

Hi Jill,

Because you are likely scaling the team quickly after your recent funding, here's an article that provides 5 best practices for Enterprise Sales teams to make sure they're spending time on the right customers.

The article describes how to target the 25% of leads that are legitimate to minimize the grunt work for your SDRs.

Hope this is helpful,

Meghan

P.S. If you'd like to learn more insights, please connect with me on LinkedIn where I share my favorite articles on best practices.

Email Day Eighteen

Subject: Your sales process monitoring

Hi Jill,

I often see Sales Ops folks, much like yourself, having trouble achieving visibility into their siloed sales tools; [example 1, example 2, etc.] The inability to have full visibility often times slows the sales cycle, causing a lot of time being spent running reports.

[Relevant company], for example, was able to help collect, centralize, and visualize their data in Salesforce reports to proactively see the highest-performing content and share the best material with their team. As a result, they reduced their sales cycle by 15% in one quarter.

Jill, do you think this could have value at [your company?]

Cheers,

Meghan

Email Day Twenty One

Subject: Just not interested or busy?

Hi Jill,

Please excuse my polite persistence. With your Series C announcement, there must be many priorities you're juggling. If you are just busy, I'm happy to reach out when the timing is better – please let me know.

Jill, is there anyone on your team that would benefit from learning more from some of the insights I've shared with you?

Cheers,

Meghan

CALL TO ACTION: If anyone opens your email within 5 minutes do the following:

STEP 1 **45-60 second research + keep researching while dialing**

- Visit profile

- Look for recent 3 jobs

- Read what they like (references they received)

- Check interests and publications

- Check recent blog posts and social media activity

STEP 2 **Place a call (remember they're thinking "Who are you, why are you calling, what's in it for me?)**

Hello Mary – this is Mike, how are you?

Doing all right...Who is this?

My name is Mike from XYZ I am calling you because you are the VP of Marketing at Acme, right?

Yes. What is this about?

Based on your ... [reference your relevant research]... I sent you a link to a use-case...

And I was wondering if you had an opportunity to take a look at it?

Yes I am looking at it right now!

Would you like me to save you some time of reading it all and give you the cliff notes?

Yes why not...

BEST PRACTICES

- **DO** provide customer-centric messaging – write about them, not about "I."

- **DO** personalize, and if possible HYPER-personalize – NO ONE wants to read SPAM.

- DO keep it short and sweet.

- DO consider how it appears on a mobile device (65% of emails are read on mobile).

- DO develop different cadences for different personas (a VP of Sales cares about different things than a Sales Director, a Marketer, etc.).

- DO be creative, and use your personality to your advantage.

- **DO NOT** abuse GIF files of cool cats. This fad has passed.

- DO use A/B testing to see what works and what doesn't.

- DO switch up your cadences. For example, you should use a different cadence for an INBOUND vs. a COLD OUTBOUND. If they come inbound, they are warm and interested in information, so you can reach out more frequently.

- DO use finesse. Based on your target persona's specific buying preference, you may need more phone calls, or fewer. Here's some guidelines to get started:

  - **Introduction:** Send a couple lines to your prospect to introduce yourself and how she will benefit from what your company does. Remember, customers buy benefits, not features.

  - **Provide Value:** Share a piece of content that educates your customer and makes her better at her job.

  - **Offer Help:** Because you know her persona, ask the prospect what her goals are in relation to the top 3 benefits you've helped people like her accomplish. Share one more piece of valuable content.

- **Engage for Feedback:** Ask about the content you sent over – was it helpful? You've now established yourself with some credibility.

- **The Ask:** You've earned it after providing a bit of value. Do you have 15 minutes for a call next Tuesday afternoon?

- **DO NOT** pursue a person hard with email/call as they will NOT accept your LinkedIn request.

- **DO** adhere to local culture. In Europe, it is common to not accept a LinkedIn request until you meet the person or build a strong relationship.

- **DO** visit someone's profile – this is considered an outbound touch.

- **DO NOT** pursue a person on personal social channels (Facebook!) – this is considered stalking.

2.3 Measuring Engagement

By monitoring our engagement, we are able to make data-driven decisions. Let's first establish what your target open rate looks like for a decent outbound campaign – fill in your target open and reply rates for your outbound emailing below:

Open Rate	Reply Rate
......%	......%

In order to achieve this, you need to A/B test. A/B testing means that you compare two similar emails – they are exactly the same, except for only one item in the email. Most commonly, one of the following: The subject, The body, The call-to-action.

Here are a few potential conclusions from some sample A/B test results, according to Mark Kosoglow:

- **55% OPEN AND 4.0% REPLY** Subject is great, body is not driving action. A/B test body.

- **25% OPEN AND 2.5% REPLY** Subject line is killing effectiveness of body. A/B test subject.

- **30% OPEN AND 2.0% REPLY** Scrap and start over.

2.4 Prospecting Around Events

I. Different kinds of events

Table 3 Event Prospecting

Activity	Small Social Event (up to ~20 attendees)	Online Webinar (up to ~1,000 sign-ups)	Regional Event (up to ~300 attendees)
Online Registration	Via a blog post ~10 days before the event.	Via a blog post two business days before the event.	Via a dedicated landing page >30 days before the event.
Invitations	Bulk of people sign up on the Sunday before. Needs to be hyper-personalized and use email/phone to invite.	Bulk of people sign up 24 hours before event. Use of "influencers" via social media.	Bulk of people sign up 1-2 weeks before event. Mass emailing, and hyper-personalization of influencers and speakers.

Activity	Small Social Event (up to ~20 attendees)	Online Webinar (up to ~1,000 sign-ups)	Regional Event (up to ~300 attendees)
Confirmation	As they sign up • 48 hours before • the morning of	At sign-up • 15 minutes before	At sign-up • 1 week before event • 1 day before event
The Event	Expect 50-60% to show up.	Expect 20-30% to attend (most people want the recording).	Expect 50-60% if it is free; if it is paid, expect 80-90% attendance.
Follow-up: Thank You for attending	If the event is on Thursday, follow up on Sunday. Follow-up should include key takeaways from the event.	Within 2-3 hours following the event, send the recording of the webinar.	Do not follow up immediately, as people need to catch up on their email while they were out of the office, etc. Give it a few days.
Follow-up: Sorry you missed it	As soon as the event is done (hours).	As soon as the event is done (hours).	As soon as the event is done (hours).
Follow Up: blog for those who did not attend	Update blog post within hours; resocialize.	Within hours	Within hours
Social Media	Not as much as you think, as you generally get the wrong attendees for small events (e.g., job seekers). Primarily a blog post and personalized LinkedIn invitations.	Go all-out on social media: • Blog post on LinkedIn • Twitter invitations • Facebook invitations • Status updates	Go all-out on social media.

REGISTRATION	Open a registration page, create a welcoming landing page, easily communicated through social media.
INVITATION	A list of identified prospects, customers or customers are invited:

        a. If it is a smaller event, hyper-relevant emails and phone calls are used to invite.

        b. If it is a larger audience, social media can be used.

CONFIRMATION	Qualified attendees are developed before, during, and after the event.
THE EVENT	Prospects attend the event.
FOLLOW-UP	Following attendance, we follow-up with everyone (attendants, no shows, etcetera).

II. Invitation process

There are different ways of registering attendees to consider:

BLOG We highly recommend using a blog post to start the conversation. At the top, middle, and bottom, invite customers to join the conversation at the event with a sign-up button.

EVENTBRITE Best to use Eventbrite for events with larger sign-ups, and/or if a fee is charged.

MEETUP Best for informal get-togethers, NOT good for paid professional events.

LANDING PAGE Best for events with a 1-2 day agenda, speakers details, etc.; may embed an Eventbrite invite.

EMAIL/CALENDAR INVITE Send out email invitations, followed by a calendar invite. The use of the calendar invite has proven to drive up attendance significantly.

INVITATION PLAY 1 SingleTap™

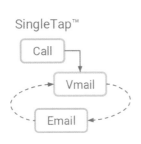

- Place a call.

- Leave a voicemail referring to the email.

- Email referring to the voicemail that provides value.

INVITATION PLAY 2 DoubleTap™

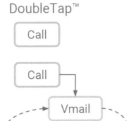

- Place a call.

- Wait 10 minutes.

- Place another call.

- Leave a voicemail referring to the email.

- Email referring to the voicemail that provides value.

SocialTap™

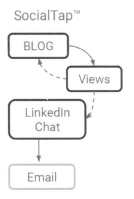

- Write a blog post on the event.
- Monitor views/shares/likes and comments.
- Send a LinkedIn message.
- Move to Email.

Send the invitation

The invitation to the event needs to be something that appears on their calendars. Most people believe that, if they signed up via Eventbrite, Meetup or other, they will get notified automatically. These invites often do require them to opt-in to get it on their calendar. Why take the risk? Instead, send anyone that signed up a separate *Calendar Invite.*

The invite needs to contain valuable info, such as location, parking, etc. The goal of the invitation is to:

- Secure attendance.
- Act as a "briefing" in case the invite is forwarded inside the company.
- Provide practical details about the value of the event.

EXAMPLE: A sample invitation is below:

DESIGN YOUR SALES ENGINE FOR HYPER-GROWTH
Winning By Design Breakfast Briefing @ Stanford
October 13 - 7:30AM - 9:30AM

PARKING: RESERVED PARKING PROVIDED – Tresidor Lot (L-39), just in front of the Stanford Faculty Club. Posted spaces will be numbers 92 – 134

Keynote: XXXXX EmCap
Asks the question: "Is Enterprise Hyper-Growth the New Normal?"

Session: Jacco van der Kooij, Winning By Design
Shares: "How To Design a Hyper-Growth Sales Organization." In this SaaS CEO insider session, you will learn about the impact of recent developments in sales and the preparation companies need for 2016 rapid growth.

- Why sales organizations fail to scale.

- How this will impact your company.

- What prescribed actions you can take, and why you need to take them now.

Practicals:
- Breakfast provided at 7:30 a.m.
- Dress code is business casual
- In case of issues, please call Michelle at 123 456-7890

Forward invite: If you know of anyone else who can benefit from attending, please feel free to forward: Link to invite.

III. Confirm attendance

SingleTap™

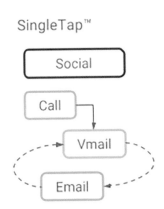

The confirmation is low-profile to make sure you do not overwhelm.

- Visit their LinkedIn Profile.
- Place a call.
- Leave a voicemail referring to the email.
- Email referring to the voicemail that provides value.

There are three kinds of confirmations that each give a different opportunity/advantage.

EXAMPLE EMAIL #1 Upon registration ask them to have their peers join:

Subject: Your Confirmation / Invite a friend

Hello Mary,

Congratulations! We secured you a seat. You can find the confirmation details below. Do let us know if you know of anyone else you think can benefit from these kind of insights.

Looking forward to seeing you!

Mike

EXAMPLE EMAIL #2 Start the conversation before the event starts

Subject: See you on Thu / Great article that makes the point!

Hello Mary,

Thought you'd appreciate this article that talks about "Inside Sales Organizations are Growing by 300%." In particular that they see them move to new markets such as Dallas. <LINK>

Suzanne from ACME Corp will join us and share her experience.

See you on Thursday; call me if anything comes up 123-456-7890

Mike

The extra asset provides increased engagement, and shows which customers are more interested, even if they miss the session at the last moment.

EXAMPLE EMAIL #3 Right before the event provide a helping hand

Subject: Single Click Dial in for your convenience

Hello Mary,

If you are anything like me, you probably looking for the dial-in numbers, so you may find this single click to join helpful:

Click*: 123 456-7890,,98766542

Cheers,

Mike

 **PRO TIP** Notice the 2 commas between the dial-in number and the login code – that creates a single click to dial-in if they're calling in from a smartphone. This removes a huge common frustration and will be greatly appreciated by your customers.

– DAN SMITH

IV. During the event

Use your social media:

- **Set up your tweets** (following Social Selling certification).

- **Take pictures of the event** that show the educational nature of the event; you can later tweet these pictures, or post them on social media. DO NOT make references to "you missing out."

- **Take detailed notes, and write a follow-up post** with key takeaways on behalf of your customers.

SocialTap™

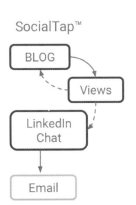

DURING EVENT PLAY 1 SocialTap™

- Write a blog post on the event.

- Monitor views/shares/likes and comments

- Send a LinkedIn message.

- Move to Email.

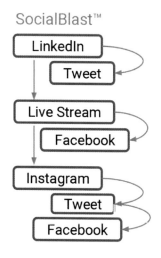

SocialBlast™

- LinkedIn
  - Tweet
- Live Stream
  - Facebook
- Instagram
  - Tweet
  - Facebook

DURING EVENT PLAY 2 SocialBlast™

- Build an audience on LinkedIn and Share on LinkedIn.

- Build a following on Twitter and Tweet using a #.

- Launch a Live Stream during the event.

- Share on Facebook.

- Take and share pictures during the event.

- Tweet the pictures.

- Facebook the pictures.

V. Following up on the event

EVENT FOLLOW-UP: **Blog Post Force Multiplier Play**

Following up on the event is where the rubber meets the road; there are three key activities here:

STEP 1 Write a blog post

A blog post that summarizes your takeaways allows you to make the event last forever. It can also help create a series of new leads. As you can see in the image here, there are 1,199 views on this post. More importantly, there are 210 likes. These are people you can now "qualify" and reach out to.

CEO+1
Sales hyper growth in 2016

Jacco van der Kooij
Help SaaS companies scale sales. Author of
Blueprints for a SaaS Sales Organization.

Edit post | View stats

CEO Breakfast on Hyper Growth

Oct 14, 2015 | 1,199 views ○ 210 Likes ⌐ 24 Comments in f

No longer is your outbound a cold call! Now you have used an event, which generated a lot of insight, that you turned into a blog post – and that, in turn, generates leads 24/7.

You see the impact?

STEP 2 **Follow up directly**

When you follow up, you need to be timely. Sometimes, this means you have to do it right away (e.g., online webinar), and sometimes early the following week. Best practice shows that follow-up on a Friday afternoon/Saturday is a waste of effort. Sunday night and Tuesday mornings show better engagement in the follow-up.

The follow-up should be HYPER-PERSONALIZED for the smaller event (up to 300 attendees). Meaning, every person should get a personal "thank you" note for attending. Even better, give them something of additional value for their effort!

STEP 3 **Follow up with those who missed it**

Those who missed it are often the ones who are of most interest, because they were too busy to attend. You can qualify who signed up but missed the event, and is a real lead, and create a personalized note:

Subject: Do a 1-1 session instead?

Hello Jennifer – Since you could not make it last Thursday, but did sign up, do you want me to schedule a 1-1 session instead? Here is a link that shares the key takeaways from the session – Jane.

Do you notice how we got to the point? We are "mirroring" the behavior of the customer – so busy that they could not make it. Hence, we keep the message short and sweet.

FOLLOW-UP EVENT PLAY 1 SingleTap™

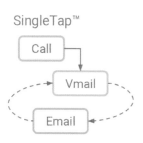

SingleTap™

- Place a call.
- Leave a voicemail referring to the email.
- Email referring to the voice mail that provides value.

FOLLOW-UP EVENT PLAY 2 BlogTap™

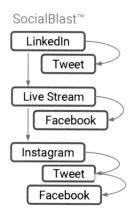

SocialBlast™

- Write a blog post.
- Share with:
  - Attendees
  - No shows
  - Anyone
- See who shares the blog.
- Qualify and reach out with LinkedIn message:
  - Those who shared the post.
  - Those who the post was shared with.
  - Those who liked/viewed etc.
- Follow-up with LinkedIn message with additional insights.

Execution of these sequence is the responsibility of the Development Representative. Time, effort, intent, and approach all heavily influence the attendance:

- **TIME:** Different events have different timelines. Sometimes you have to rush and respond instantly, while at other times you have to hurry up and wait.

- **INTENT:** Your attendees can sense your intent. If it is to sell them something, you will not have high attendance. Your intent must be to educate, inform, advise, and provide insight.

- **APPROACH:** How are you going to go about it – a mass email to get broader awareness, or a Hyper-relevant message? Each of these has pros and cons to consider depending on the event.

- **EFFORT:** Of all the things that we do not control, it must be mentioned that we have seen many cases where the outcome is directly related to the effort put into it. Hard work delivers results.

Event plays along the event process™

Organizing an event is a great way to generate leads for your business.

The principle behind this is that you are GIVING/SHARING information during the event; this attracts the right audience, which wishes to invest time in LEARNING. The importance is to have people become aware of the event and the valuable insights being shared. Here is a proven sequence to make sure the event is a success.

3 Target-based Prospecting

For every complex problem, there is a simple solution....

...and it's always wrong

– H. L. Mencken

Target Account Selling (TAS) is an approach in which you address several people in the same account with a hyper-relevant message. Over the years, this required a lot of research and understanding of the account, and thus it could only be applied to the top 5-10 accounts. Account Based Marketing (ABM) uses the same philosophy. TAS is the approach from the Sales discipline, and ABM from the Marketing discipline. TAS traditionally has been very unscalable due to the Hyper-relevant approach. ABM is turning the TAS approach into a repeatable process. Account-based Prospecting focuses only on the prospecting part of ABM.

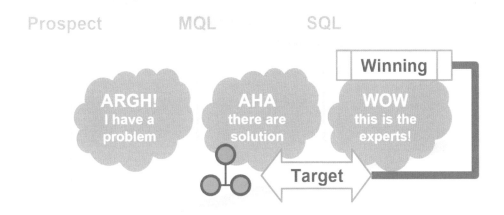

Figure 18: Targeting an account and winning

The ABM approach is typically for enterprise-level sales teams. It was first introduced in the mid-1990s to trend away from Lead Based Marketing, or mass marketing, focused on driving a high volume of leads.

Just like you learned earlier about outbound sequencing from 1:1 vs. 1:many, the goal of TAS and ABM is to help a few customers extensively rather than helping as many new customers as possible.

The high level of sophistication of tools, content, and skills to make TAS work makes this process profitable for high-ACV deals only.

Key steps of Account-Based Marketing are:

STEP 1 **Pick a list of target accounts.** These are companies that are likely to be a great fit for your solution based on size, use-case, and business need.

STEP 2 **Identify the roles and map to accounts.** Focus on the teams that would likely evaluate the solution together across the four major hierarchies (i.e. CxO to User).

STEP 3 **Research (in depth!) the account and obtain contact data.** Find alert events, executive priorities, and individuals who have published content on a relevant subject within the organization.

STEP 4 **Create a person-based value proposition.** Typically, the more senior the title, the more strategic their role. Find value props that match their day-to-day priorities in order to attract their attention and provide value.

STEP 5 **Design Interactions.** Implement a series of engagements that shares insights aligned with what you have researched (Step 3), and do it specific to each role (Step 4).

STEP 6 **Determine your account engagement play.** Engage in a conversation in context of their situation, phase etc.

STEP 7 **Measure and Improve.** Do more of what works. Stop doing what doesn't work.

3.1 Account-based Prospecting

Tier 1 Accounts (Tens)	Tier 2 Accounts (Hundreds)
These are the top accounts and will be pursued by Hyper-relevant messaging to the individual, the account, and the problem. This should be a short list of accounts.	This is your next tier of accounts. You can pursue them with a personalized approach, but generic to title/problem, etc.
Target Market:	**Target Market:**
Example Account/Use-case:	**Example Account/Use-case:**
1.	1. ....
2.	2. ....
3.	3. ....
4.	4. ....
5.	5. ....
6.	6. ....
7.	7. ....
8.	8. ....
9.	9. ....
10.	10. ....

I. Identify roles

A buying center brings together all members of an organization who are involved in the buying process, *regardless of the position they are in*. Role-based mapping recognizes the users as equal in the process to that of a CEO/Gatekeeper. It can go up/down the organization and across siloed parts of the organization.

Role	Description
INITIATOR	Makes a request to purchase a product or service or recognizes the problem; with this action, they start the decision-making process. e.g., maintenance manager.
DECIDER	Makes the actual purchase decision. Typically, they don't have or need formal authority, but have sufficient weight within the buying team to decide if a service/product will be purchased.
BUYER	Selects the suppliers and manages the buying process such that the necessary products are acquired. Also called purchasing manager.
INFLUENCER	Contributes to the formulation and determination of the specifications of the product or service. The influencer evaluates and recommends which potential supplier satisfies the specific needs of the organization.
USER	People who actually use the product or service. They are not always involved in the buying process, but have a critical role in the feedback and evaluation of the performance of the good that has been purchased.
GATEKEEPER	Controls the flow of information in and out of the company, buying center, and teams.

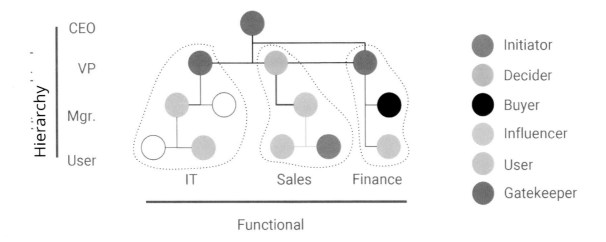

Figure 19: Hierarchical persona-based decision tree

This diagram demonstrates the functional groups vs. hierarchy; this is useful to target each of these groups with content over time. For example, the User group in this case is the "sales" team. They may be targeted well before the "IT" team. You can now design 3 different campaigns:

- Sales ➔ User data/best practices

- IT ➔ Security and Scaling

- Finance ➔ Spending, RoI and cost comparison vs. competitors

II. Research account

We need to identify the right contacts inside a targeted company.

STEP 1 **What are the sample titles of your key contacts within a customer?**
(e.g., Chief Customer Officer, Creative Talent Manager, Inside Sales Manager, etc.)

- .... [Title]

- .... [Title]

- .... [Title]

- .... [Title]

- .... [Title]

STEP 2 **Develop an understanding of each of the roles identified**

Create a description of the persona by researching their LinkedIn profile in detail:

- Who are they (hobbies, personality, family status, etc.).

- What content do they like (video, white paper, books, etc.).

- Where do they get their information (LinkedIn, Quora, newsletters, LinkedIn groups, Twitter, etc.).

Example	Now Your Turn (go to their LinkedIn profile)
Jody J @ ACME	Name: ....
• VP Marketing	• ....
• Female mid 40s	• ....
• On LinkedIn and Twitter	• ....
• Loves video content and Infographics	• ....
• Tweets about 4-5/week	• ....
• Part of LinkedIn group x, y and z	• ....
• Video on YouTube: xxxxx	• ....
• Blog posts on topics: yyyyyy	• ....

STEP 3 **Obtain contact information**

Obtaining contact data is not as hard as it seems. Google Chrome extensions like Email Hunter (https://emailhunter.co/) provide you with a customer's email address by checking the database of email syntaxes. Also check www.mailtester.com to double check or find others.

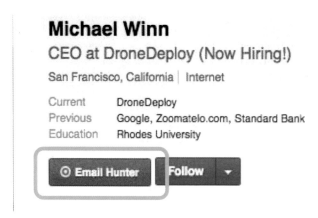

As we map this over time, you see how the decision evolves and roams through the organization up and down decision trees of different functional groups.

Step by step through the decision tree

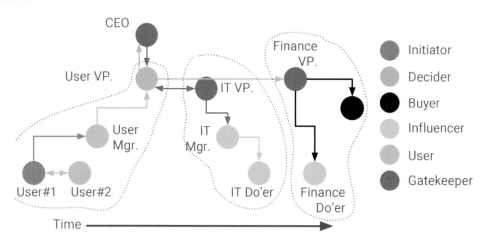

Figure 20: Consensus persona decision tree

1. Enthusiastic user #1 runs into a problem and finds a solution.

2. He runs it by his colleague, user #2, who loves it also.

3. They get the User Manager to participate in the trial.

4. User Manager sees the benefits from the reports she is getting and she runs it up to the VP.

5. The VP sees the financial benefits, but is also happy to hear his team is excited about it; so, he does not have to worry about "retaining" them.

6. He runs a snapshot value prop by the CEO with the impact it has on the business.

7. The CEO says to make sure that IT is OK with it, and that Finance has it in the budget.

8. User VP asks IT VP to check it.

9. IT VP delegates it to the IT Manager.

10. IT Manager delegates it to the IT Do'er, who runs the analysis to make sure it runs on the "stack" and it obeys "security regulation," and then gives the thumbs up to IT Manager, who in turns gives the thumbs up to the IT VP.

11. IT VP lets User VP know.

12. At the same time, the User VP asked the Finance VP how the budget is doing.

13. Finance VP delegates to the Finance Do'er.

14. Finance Do'er runs the numbers and says it fits.

15. Finance VP lets User VP know.

16. User VP tasks buyer to "buy."

17. Buyer googles and finds 2 competitors; asks User Manager to run a trial and obtain pricing from all three vendors. To start the sales process...

III. Role-based value prop

Next we need to develop valuable content: This can be separated into "account-specific content" that is valuable across the entire company, and "role-specific content."

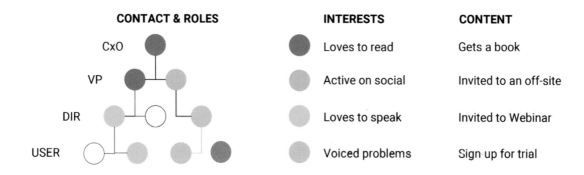

Figure 21: Role-based interests and content to drive engagement

IV. Account-specific content map

Based on your research, identify the top 3 problems and create 2-3 assets per problem that you can share with the account.

	Role And Value Prop	Content Related to This Problem
1	INITIATOR / Change the way we work	See a visual video on the benefits
2		Want to know they were heard, see a resolution
3		
4		

V. Account engagement plays

ABM PLAY #1 **Startup Play**

Goal: In this play, we know that companies that receive funding scale their sales teams. This impacts everyone:

- CEO who wants to see growth potential.

- VP Sales who needs to recruit a sales team.

- Inside Sales Manager who needs data/report on best practices.

- Sales team that probably wants tools/skills to help scale with existing resources.

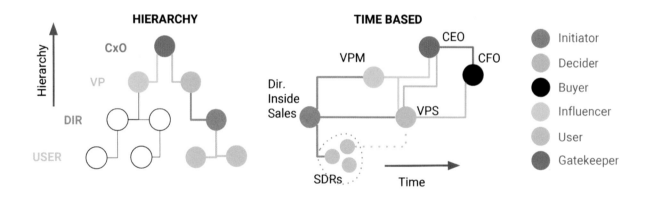

Figure 22: ABM Startup Play

VI. Plays defined as a function of content

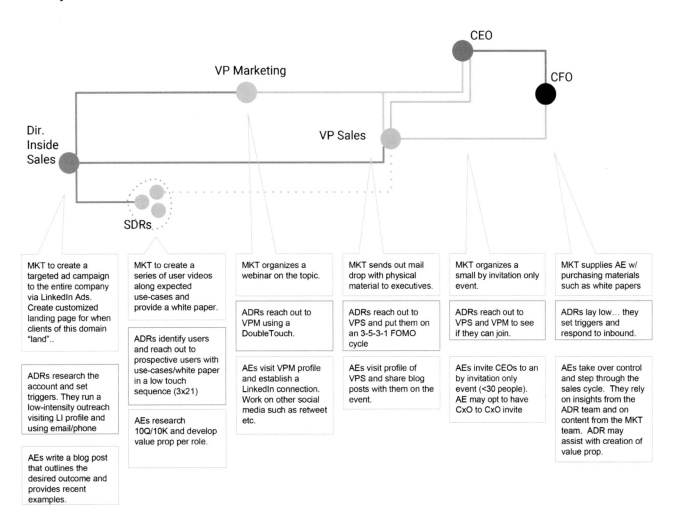

Figure 23: ABM Play by function of content

VII. Perform account plays

Engaging with people inside the account means that you provide your insight in a friendly way (not SPAMMING) through a variety of methods, outlined below:

Ways To Engage	Description
Outbound call/ email	Reach out via a direct email and/or phone call (described further below); this is the most common way to reach out. You have the following to consider: • Reach out to **individuals within an account** (Jenn the VP of Marketing). • Reach out to a **group within an account** (marketing team). • Reach out to a group across accounts (CMOs). As you reach out, you can use either: • Hyper-relevant 1-1. • Group personalized 1-few. And you can choose which method: • **1-Dimensional**: Reach out multiple times to an individual in one day. • **2-Dimensional**: Reach out to group of people with one value prop across multiple days. • **3-Dimensional**: Reach out to different groups of people with different value props across multiple days.
Social engagement	Visiting their LinkedIn profile, commenting on their post, sharing an article, inviting them to connect, etc.

Ways To Engage	Description
Invite them to an event	Think of a webinar, a social gathering, an industry event, etc. You can organize events in various ways: ● **Account-Specific:** Gather people from within the account; very useful to expand reach within an account. ● **Industry-Specific**: Gather specialists across key accounts to discuss industry topics. Very useful mixing prospects with customers. ● **Title-Specific:** Bring a specific role (CMOs) together to discuss issues they care about at their level. Very useful to gain executive coverage within your account portfolio. ● **Problem-Specific:** Discussing an issue (such as "Safe Harbor"); very useful to break open an account. Reaching out to your audience with the request to join an event is a great way to start a meaningful relationship.
Mail	Mailing a relevant book, a personal invite, a handwritten note, a Starbucks gift card to grab a coffee, etc. Very effective, especially in combination with an event. Note: Increasingly, companies are not allowed to receive gifts and/or cannot exceed $50 cumulative over a year (including coffee/lunch). *My personal favorite for an SDR performing account-based development is to send a personal handwritten note on a simple white stock card.*
Your idea	What is your personal experience that has shown to work well?

EXERCISE: **Put the pieces together to create account plays**

ABM PLAY #2 ....

STEP 1 **Pick your key account** ....

STEP 2 **Identify the roles**

Role	Name(S)	Research
INITIATOR	....	....
DECIDER	....	....
BUYER	....	....
INFLUENCER	....	....
USER	....	....
GATEKEEPER	....	....

STEP 3 **Research (in depth!) and obtain contact data**

STEP 4 **Create a person-based value proposition**

Role	Pain Points	Simple Value Prop
INITIATOR	....	....
DECIDER	....	....
BUYER	....	....
INFLUENCER	....	....
USER	....	....
GATEKEEPER	....	....

STEP 5 **Design Interaction**

Role	Content / Outreach	Cadence
INITIATOR	....	....
DECIDER	....	....
BUYER	....	....
INFLUENCER	....	....
User	....	....
GATEKEEPER	....	....

STEP 6 **Determine your account engagement play mapping roles to content over time**

Role	First Do This	Then This	Then This	Finally This
INITIATOR	....	....	....	....
DECIDER	....	....	....	....
BUYER	....	....	....	....
INFLUENCER	....	....	....	....
USER	....	....	....	....
GATEKEEPER	....	....	....	....

3.2 Alert-based Selling

Alert-based selling helps you prospect and qualify by leveraging tools to do a lot of the work for you.

In this section, you will learn the best practices for prospecting systems, and the type of information you can use in your daily routine to find the right people at the right time.

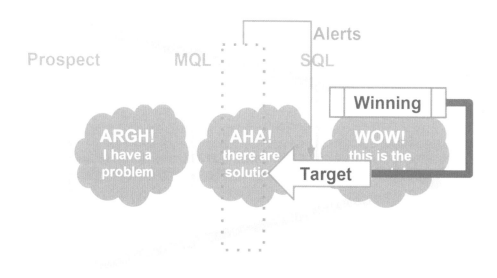

Figure 24: Setting alerts on an account

Here's a quick overview of Alert-based lead generation:

1. A target account list is received.

2. The Development Rep identifies the key events, and sets Alerts on various websites, such as a saved search for new hires on LinkedIn, or notifications for new questions asked on Quora.

3. The Development Rep receives notifications as the Alerts go off.

4. The Development Rep takes action and performs an outbound call, email or social interaction but *with a Hyper-relevant approach.*

5. Prospect expresses interest to learn more.

6. Following qualification, the Development Rep sets up the next steps.

The principles of Alert-based lead generation

Alert-based lead generation relates to customers who are taking an action that is visible on the internet. By responding to that Alert, we're avoiding a cold outbound.

- Alert actions often require timely response; depending on the alert, this can be from minutes (respond to a question on Quora) to days (congratulations on a job promotion on LinkedIn).

- Responses to alerts need to be hyper-personalized.

- This is an ideal way to use advanced tools.

- Alerts must have a high signal-to-noise ratio. For example, someone's anniversary is a noisy signal, but a new Ideal Customer Profile (ICP) joining your target account is a high signal.

I. Identifying Alerts

Identify the alerts for your business. The types of alerts you set up are used to start conversations to make your cold calls turn warm.

Examples of effective alerts:

- Raised a new round of funding.

- New executive or board member hired.

- Moved into new office.

- Open positions.

Here are a few examples of alerts you can use:

- Google Alerts

- IFTTT

- LinkedIn Saved Searches

- LinkedIn Pulse (happens automatically in your news feed)

- LInkedIn Sales Navigator

- Twitter generated Alert (e.g., TweetDeck)

- Quora alerts

- Specific vertical portals, such as Crunchbase or Mattermark for the VC industry.

II. Alert engagement plays

Next, a few examples of how to practically use alerts.

ALERT PLAY #1 **Google Alerts**

Set a Google Alert for accounts you are targeting, industries you are involved in, etc. You can set the delivery time of the alerts to the day and time that matches up with your "social media" time blocks on your schedule. This way, your alerts become the automatic "timer" for you to stop calling and get started on your alert work.

Figure 25: Setting up Google Alert

EXERCISE: **Write down the Google Alerts you should to set:**

Company	Industry	Technology
....	....	....
....	....	....
....	....	....
....	....	....
....	....	....

Alert-based plays

ALERT PLAY #2 **LinkedIn Sales Navigator - Save Search**

STEP 1 **Click on Lead Builder**

STEP 2 **Create your search until you have a reasonable size (hundreds)**

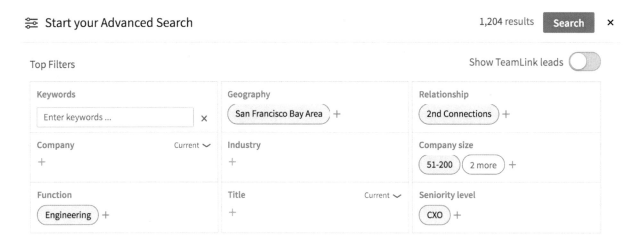

STEP 3 **Save the search - and you will receive weekly lead updates that match your "Alert"**

Figure 26: Setting up an alert in LinkedIn Sales Navigator

EXERCISE: **Write down the LinkedIn saved searches: Create four saved searches**

Criteria	Criteria 1 (Title)	Criteria 2 (Business)
1	VP, Dir, Human Resources	Bay Area, >500 employees, Media
2		
3		
4		

If you have set up LinkedIn properly (see *The SaaS Sales Method Fundamentals: How to Have Customer Conversations)*, and you are sharing content and building your network, then it's time to switch on LinkedIn Pulse. It provides daily updates about what is going on in your network. The key for this to occur is to:

- Connect with your prospects, and customers on LinkedIn.

- Follow the companies on LinkedIn (see below).

Figure 27: Following a target account in LinkedIn

- Minimize following people who create a lot of noise (some people create so many updates each week that your customer news is overwhelmed by only their updates).

Once you set up these alerts, you will receive daily/weekly updates like the below...

Research platform UserZoom Technologies raises
$34 million to improve online experience on business

...allowing you to send a message like the following:

Subject: Congratulations!

Julia, congratulations on the funding round! You must have worked hard on this over the past few months. High five, and do let me know if there is anything we can do to help!

Michael

3.3 CxO-based Outreach

In this approach, you are using a common connection to reach out to the decision maker. For example, your own CEO may know their GM/CFO. This means that you have to write a message for your own CEO to forward to the their GM/CFO – who forwards it to the decision maker.

Although this goes through many steps, it often goes extremely fast – executives tend to forward these message promptly. But this requires that you perform proper research, put that into an email for your CEO so that it's really simple for him to send along.

CXO PLAY 1 Contact CxO using a reference

Great for these situation:

- Platform sale
- CxO outreach
- Leverage your VC
- When it's unclear who owns

Pros:

- Obtain a quick Yes/No
- Often an internal referral

Cons:

- Requires deep research
- Time-consuming
- May feel resistance upon further entry into the account

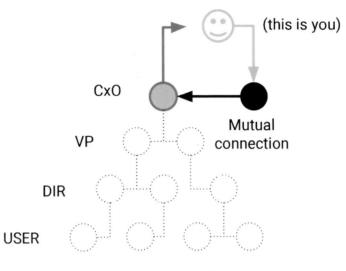

Figure 28: CxO Play

How to ghost write a message for your CEO

`STEP 1` **Perform research to identify relevance 10K/Q, YouTube, Twitter, Google, press release etc.**

`STEP 2` **Write your email in the RRR format**

    `R` Relevance   Open with research and/or a reference, show that this email is specifically for them.

    `R` Reward   Offer value, such as a link to valuable insights, a relevant blog post, etc.

    `R` Request   State one clear ask.

`STEP 3` **Subject – Curiosity gap, not click bait**

Remember to avoid generic or bland "marketing-esque" subject lines. Instead, create subject lines that spark curiosity and are relevant to the body of the message. Always test your subject lines.

One way to start is to Pick 1 or 2 words from each `R` to make it your subject

`STEP 4` **Send it to your CEO for review/edit**

- Include the customer's full name and email address, company, relevance, and research.

- Provide one clear goal you'd like to establish.

- Cc: the Executive Admin.

- Include customer's LinkedIn link (ditto) so your CEO can check who this is sent to/mutual connections.

- Include customer link to Twitter profile so your CEO can check on character/identity/tone.

{{CEO}} – Can you please review/edit and send this note? – Jacco

Who: <customer name>, <email address> is the SVP of Corp Dev (LI) (Twitter)

Company: Stores, protects, manages info and assets for 94% of F500 with HW, services, and SW.

Relevance: In the middle of what they call the Modernization Initiative (See 10 Q), a plan that calls for certain organizational realignments to reduce overhead costs, particularly in developed markets, in order to optimize selling, general and administrative cost structure, and to support investments to advance the growth strategy.

Research: Extensive HR Program: See Use-case; <Link>

Goal: Get the SVP to intro you to their CMO (LI Link) and/or CHRO (LI Link).

<First name>,

It has been a long time. I hope you are doing well. Given your recent acquisition of <AAA>, the key competitive wins and being named<BBB>, it looks like you are knocking it out of the park. Congratulations!

My sales director shared that <XXX> and <YYY> on your team are evaluating <your company name>. That is fantastic! I trust <AE> and <SDR> are taking good care of them.

Given you are looking at my company, I would love to take the opportunity to reconnect with you. Also, <AE> mentioned you might be interested in learning how to set up _____. I would be glad to share some best practices with you.

<First name>, considering you are tied up with the ____ conference this week, how does your schedule look for early next week to have a call?

Best regards,

<first name>

P.S. Here's a <<insert something of incredible value to the customer such as market research>>

STEP 4 **Apply best practices**

- DO Keep it short! Half as long, twice as powerful.

- DO show relevance right away/show you have done your research.

- DO optimize for mobile phone. Make effective use of the Subject: and the first 50 characters.

- **DO NOT** Start every sentence with "I." Make it about their CxO, not yours.

- DO offer valuable insights.

- DO use the person's first name to draw their attention to a key point.

- **DO NOT** use exclamation points!!, **bold** or CAPITAL in your message to the customer.

- DO close with only ONE clear call to action.

- DO Use the PS. for a personal note/invite etc.

EXERCISE: Analyze message below, improve (use best practices) and rewrite to apply to your business

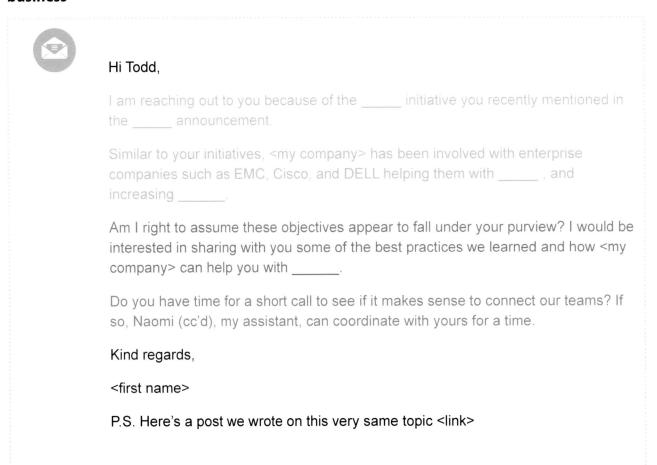

Hi Todd,

I am reaching out to you because of the _____ initiative you recently mentioned in the _____ announcement.

Similar to your initiatives, <my company> has been involved with enterprise companies such as EMC, Cisco, and DELL helping them with _____ , and increasing _____.

Am I right to assume these objectives appear to fall under your purview? I would be interested in sharing with you some of the best practices we learned and how <my company> can help you with _____.

Do you have time for a short call to see if it makes sense to connect our teams? If so, Naomi (cc'd), my assistant, can coordinate with yours for a time.

Kind regards,

<first name>

P.S. Here's a post we wrote on this very same topic <link>

...................................,

...................................,

PS: ....

Open up a Google shared doc and let everyone write one CxO message + briefing to the CEO

<CEO>,

....

....

Who: ....

....

Company: ....

....

Relevance: ....

....

....

Research: ....

....

Goal: ....

....

CXO PLAY 2 **Contact CxO - No one listened**

Great for these situations:

- When nothing else
  worked.

- When key people left the
  company.

Pros:

- Extremely effective, high
  response rate.

Cons:

- Very intrusive.

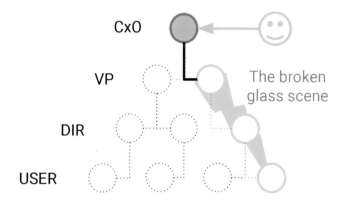

Figure 29: The scene of the crime

  IMPORTANT: This is a last ditch effort play – it *will* break glass. Seek approval from a manager. Do NOT use in ABM.

In this play, you have tried a few times throughout the organization, but no dice. It's possible that the target organization doesn't completely understand the impact of your service. Or they're not willing to. Or they are simply too busy. In this approach, you reach out directly to the CEO using your previous attempts as the source of "research," and the work you have done with the competitor as a reference. It looks something like this:

Subject: Surprised to find you not interested

Dear {{CEO first name}} -

Over the past few weeks, I have reached out to Jennifer, Alan, and Mike in the marketing department to share some key insights. Unfortunately, they expressed no interest.

The reason why I am so persistent in my outreach is because I have been working closely with others in your space, such as {{Competitor name}} and {{Competitor name}} and was able to achieve meaningful results. I read in your recent blog post that you were looking for similar results.

{{First name}}, will you let me know if this is something of interest that got lost in the shuffle? It would be my pleasure to share the valuable insights with your team.

Sincerely,

Mary

Beware that you may receive some backlash from the team because you called them out, so only use this approach sparingly, and for the right kind of company. Please note that the above already reflects a proper email structure (RRR), something you can learn more about in the Outbound Emailing section.

4   Content

Content is best understood as valuable insights delivered through a variety of media. These insights act as a magnet that attract audiences for whom it is relevant. In the picture below, you will notice two kinds of insights. One that provides more insight into the problem, such as a "whiteboard video," and one that provides insight to a solution, such as a "comparison between two competing vendors."

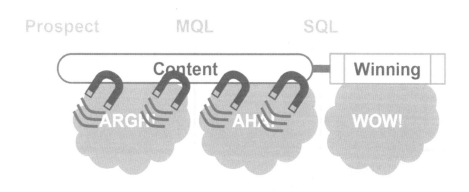

Figure 30: Targeting an account

There are different kinds of ways of distributing content:

- **Curate Content:** You review/share someone else's content.

- **Create Content:** You create your own content.

- **Content Journey:** You create a series of content you share with your customer over a set time. This is best applied to specific accounts/senior account executives.

4.1 Curate Content

When you curate, you engage with content and share it with your network. Since the people in your network trust your judgment, they value the article. This, once again, emphasizes the impact of your presence online and is why you should be so careful with maintaining it.

Curating content has two important impacts:

- You contribute your own insights to your network. This increases your value as you become a thought leader on a specific topic.

- You can curate content that your prospect has written. This is a very powerful approach, as your prospect is nudged in the most friendly way about your presence.

CONTENT CURATION PLAY **Preparation**

	Click Curation	Click+Write Curation	Proving Insight Curation
Methods of Curating	• Like • Retweet • Follow • Upvote • Share (others content)	• Share (your content) • Forward • .... • .... •	• Comment (LinkedIn) • Comment (blog) • Answer (Quora) • Congrats (LinkedIn) • .... • .... • ....

	Click Curation	**Click+Write Curation**	**Proving Insight Curation**
Action	View/Understand/ Click	Summarize a key takeaway relevant for your audience; try to avoid just "snipping" a headline.	Requires in-depth reading of the article and full understanding of the content, but in return it is most impactful on your lead generation.
Network Impact	Update evaporates quickly (mins to hrs)	Evaporates quickly (mins to hrs)	Does not evaporate, may stay for years. Will be subject to prioritization (likes, views, time, etc.).
Prospect Impact	He receives a friendly nudge in the form of an update, builds name recognition.	He receives an immediate update.	Your prospect receives an immediate update, provides you with high visibility, and often requires the person to respond to you.

STEP 1 **Measure what works**

As you start to share insights you have gathered from credible sources, you must measure performance:

- Which articles get shared the most and why?

- Which articles generate the best quality of leads?

- Who is always involved (retweets you, etc.)?

STEP 2 **Do more of what works ...**

... and stop doing what doesn't work.

STEP 3 **Write a lot of thank yous**

- Thank you for sharing

- Thank you for liking

- Thank you for your comments

- Who are my top shares this week

- Thank you for following me

- Thank you, thank you, thank you!

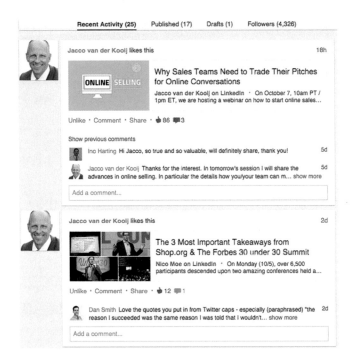

STEP 4 **Team up with a peer**

It's called "social" for a reason! Learn to recognize who has great articles that you can trust as great content when you hit like.

STEP 5 **Creating multi-touch**

So you want to create the Ultimate. You can do this by linking comments to multiple blog posts, thus creating the impression that "you are everywhere." Here's how it works:

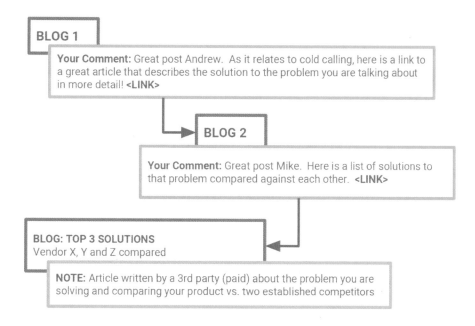

Figure 31: Social engagement examples

4.2 Create Content

Content can be used as an outbound call. Those who engage with the content can be contacted with the intent to share more valuable insights with the goal of having a conversation.

Figure 32: How to use content as an outbound call

IMPORTANT: Content-based outbound takes place primarily in the *educational* part of the customer journey:

- Argh! – I have a problem.

- Aha! – There is a solution.

Therefore, at no point in time can you "sell" during content-based outbound. You must educate. The goal is to engage a customer in an online conversation, very similar to how you'd approach a customer at a coffee shop or at a conference. You have to use your insights as the conversation starter.

EXAMPLE: **Create content (LinkedIn)**

Summarize your week's experiences; what are the problems your customers talk about?

PROBLEM 1: ....

USE-CASE STORY: ....

PROBLEM 2: ....

USE-CASE STORY: ....

PROBLEM 3: ....

USE-CASE STORY: ....

TOP 3 ISSUES EVERYONE IN _____ RUNS INTO

In the past weeks, I must have spoken to at least xx people. And they all say that they are running into the same issues.

Problem 1 _____

Mary from a large ___ in the Midwest described to me that she lacks a real practical dashboard to improve her decision-making. In her own words, she asked for: x, y and z.

Problem 2 _____

Jennifer from a large East Coast firm described to me that she runs into _____ every day. She voiced how this is causing _____

Problem 3 _____

Anshu, who is the CTO at a fast growing start-up, was speaking at ____ I caught up with him for a few minutes after and he said ____ and _____.

Does any of this resonate with you? Do you see the same or different? Love to hear from you. Please use the comments to share your point of view.

BEST PRACTICES

- DO provide VALUE by providing real insights.
- DO make your content easy to scan through.
- DO add a visual that tells the story, a picture of a real customer situation, a selfie.
- **DO NOT** use stock photography!
- DO create content yourself – if needed, take a picture of your scribbles on a whiteboard.
- DO add a few simple quotes – this makes it easy for people to tweet.
- **DO NOT** sell: "To solve this problem – contact me at xyz and I will gladly harass you."
- DO advise "I recommend following these people – x,y,z; they often talk about interesting solutions."
- DO offer links to third-party insights such as TED, HBR, industry news articles etc. (but read first!).

4.3 Content Journey

Account Executives who are running Account-based Prospecting processes need a more automated process. Similar to email outbound sequences where the same "RRR email" can go to several customers, AEs need the same kind of "content" to go to several strategic customers.

In the figure below, you will notice that comparing this to Figure 6 the emails are replaced with content.

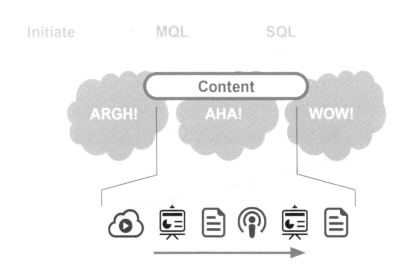

Figure 33: Provide insights along the entire customer journey

Account Executives who wish to do this for their Enterprise Accounts need to keep various people at the customer engaged over the journey. They can create a content journey, distribute it to various people, and measure engagement, allowing them to engage at the right time with the right person. Today this is done manually, but efforts are underway to launch services that provide an automated way of doing this. Folloze is one of the tools that can create such an experience.

Figure 34: Content map by persona, industry with metrics

Content journey steps:

- Leverage high quality content
- Creation of a content journey
- That's relevant to the customer
- Personalize the content
- Measure engagement
- Take action

5 Hand-off

Once a meeting has been set, we need to hand off the opportunity internally from the person responsible for the Inbound/outbound lead generation process to the person held accountable for the winning process. This step is called the "hand-off."

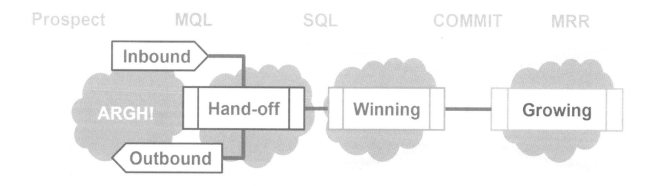

Figure 35: SDR/AE internal hand-off process

EXERCISE: **Hand-off steps**

HAND-OFF	
What is their customer's situation such as infrastructure, people, etc.	**S1** ....
	S2 ....
	S3 ....
What are the biggest problems and pains the customer experiences?	**P1** ....
	P2 ....
Relevant customer story shared	**Use-Case** ....
Do they need this by a certain date?	**Critical Event** ....
Do they need to accomplish a certain Impact	**Impact** ....

EXERCISE: **Identify the hand-off process for a WARM SQL to an AE**

STEP 1 ....

STEP 2 ....

STEP 3 ....

EXERCISE: **Identify the hand-off process for a TARGET ACCOUNT to an AE**

STEP 1 ....

STEP 2 ....

STEP 3 ....

EXERCISE: **Identify the hand-off process for a DISQUALIFIED lead?**

STEP 1 ....

STEP 2 ....

STEP 3 ....

EXAMPLE: **Letter disqualification:**

If a customer is disqualified, the average sales person may simply click Disqualify in their CRM. However, there is an opportunity to leverage the investment you made with the intent to use the DQ'd customer as a marketer.

Hi Adoni,

Thank you for your inquiry. I greatly appreciate spending time with you.

Although naturally disappointed that it did not work out this time, I did want to send you a brief note in case you have a need later on, or come across someone who can benefit from our service.

Adoni, have a great year, and do not hesitate to let me know if my network is ever of use to you.

Thank you,

Sarah-Anne

Attachment: Video link to what we do

Attachment B: Use case of a relevant customer

Summary

Key plays by the stage of the Customer Experience Funnel

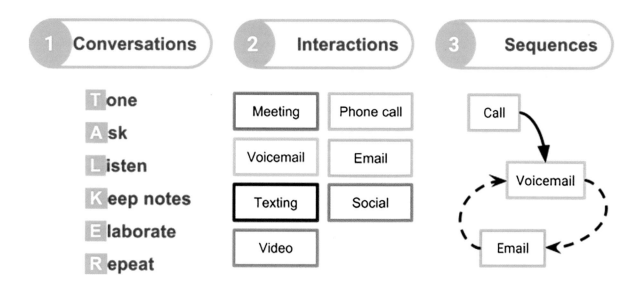

Initiate	Plays	Prepare
Inbound Play	SingleTap DoubleTap	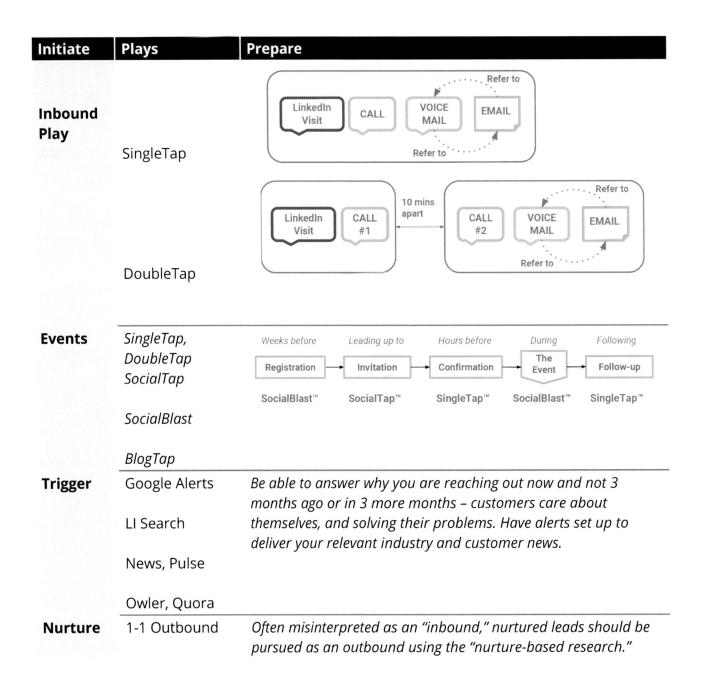
Events	*SingleTap,* *DoubleTap* *SocialTap* *SocialBlast* *BlogTap*	
Trigger	Google Alerts LI Search News, Pulse Owler, Quora	*Be able to answer why you are reaching out now and not 3 months ago or in 3 more months – customers care about themselves, and solving their problems. Have alerts set up to deliver your relevant industry and customer news.*
Nurture	1-1 Outbound	*Often misinterpreted as an "inbound," nurtured leads should be pursued as an outbound using the "nurture-based research."*

Outbound	Detail	Summary

Roles

Customer Roles
Mapped by Time or Hierarchy

1. Initiator
2. Decider
3. Buyer
4. Influencer
5. User

{ X }

6. Gatekeeper

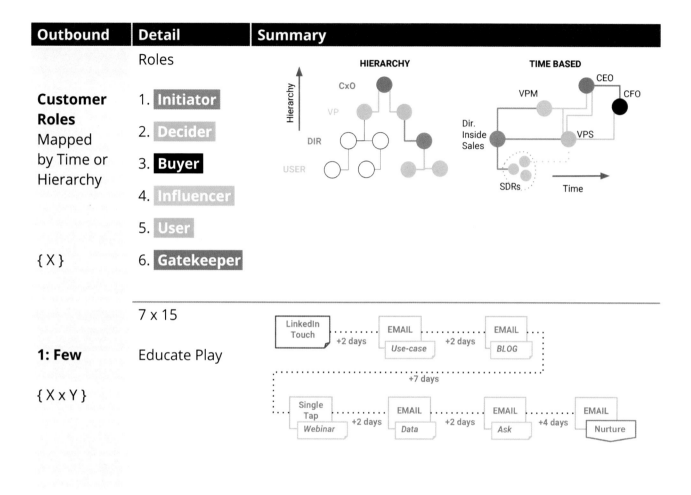

7 x 15

1: Few

Educate Play

{ X x Y }

Outbound	Detail	Summary
ABM { X x Y x Z } Target Account Selling	Enterprise Multi-channel campaigns Map accounts, and align personas with content	 *Work marketing teams, advertising campaigns and all parts of the sales team (SDR, NBS, AE) to drive conversations that are hyper-personalized. Build plays by function of content.*
Social Selling	Find relevant content Curate vs. Create	
Exercise	Creation	Write an article on customer experiences in the last weeks and the top 3 issues they all seem to struggle with! ● Mention real customers (A VP of Marketing at a Large XYZ). ● Keep it real – speak from your own voice. ● Add basic graphics, pictures, etc.

Conclusion

One of the things we often tell our clients is that doubling sales efficiently is seldom the result of just getting more quality leads, whether from marketing or from sales development activity. Instead, just making small improvements in each of the many conversion points in the sales funnel can lead to massive increases in sales. Which is just another way of saying that every little thing you do in your sales role can have an outsized impact on your results.

So, we hope that with the content and exercises in this book you have gained skills that will let you succeed as a salesperson in the constantly changing world of SaaS Sales. Of course, no amount of reading can ever substitute for practice, so we encourage you to take the key ideas in this book and test them out in your own workflow. You'll find that you will see results very quickly, and more importantly, that multiplying those changes together will have an even greater effect.

With our best,

The Winning by Design Team

Abbreviations Used in this Book

People:
AE: Account Executive
AM: Account Manager
BDR: Business Development Representative
CSM: Customer Success Manager
CEO: Chief Executive Officer
CRO: Chief Revenue Officer
CCO: Chief Customer Officer
FAE: Field Account Executive
MDR: Marketing Development Representative
PM: Product Manager
SDR: Sales Development Representative
SE: Sales Engineer, sometimes refers to a web developer
VPM: VP Marketing
VPS: VP Sales

SaaS Lead Definition:
Suspect: A person who may be interested
Prospect: A person who expresses interest
MQL: Marketing Qualified Lead, a person who expresses interest and fits the profile.
SQL: Sales Qualified Lead, person who is interested
SAL: Sales Accepted Lead
WIN: A client who commits to the service
LIVE: Client who has been onboarded

SaaS Business:
ACV: Annual Contract Value
ACRC: Annual Customer Retention Cost
ARR: Annual Recurring Revenue equal to12 times MRR
B2B: Business to Business
B4B: Business for Business
B2C: Business to Consumer
CAC: Client Acquisition Cost, the amount to acquire a single client

CR: Conversion Ratio, the amount of leads to produce one SQL
CRC: Client Retention Cost, the cost to retain a client for 12 months
CRM: Customer Relationship Management (platform)
CSM: Customer Success Management (platform)
ENT: Enterprises, companies with over 5,000 employees
LOGO: Common use term for a high-value client
LTV: Lifetime Value of a client, often between 3-5 times ACV
MAS: Marketing Automation Software (platform)
MRR: Monthly Recurring Revenue
PTC: Refers to the combined cost of (P)eople, (T)ools, and (C)ontent
RoI: Return on Investment
SaaS: Software as a Service
SC: Sales Cycle
SMB: Small to Medium Business(es) often between 50-500 employees
SME: Small to Medium Enterprise often between 500-5k employees
VSB: Very Small Business often between 2-50 employees
PRO: Prosumer, a single user who behaves like a business user
WR: Win Ratio, the number of accounts it takes to produce one WINIn the years since we published "Blueprints," we have been amazed at the response we have gotten from sales professionals in multiple fields, not just SaaS. It has been humbling!

About Winning By Design

Winning By Design was founded by Jacco Van Der Kooij with the purpose of helping SaaS companies level up their sales game in the face of radically compressed sales cycles and lower price points. We teach fundamental sales skills and combine them with process and systems to create self-teaching sales organizations.

To find out more about our offerings please visit:

www.saassalesmethod.com

Made in the USA
Las Vegas, NV
17 November 2020